Everything You Need to Know About Terrorism

by

All-American Grandma

authorHOUSE™

1663 LIBERTY DRIVE, SUITE 200
BLOOMINGTON, INDIANA 47403
(800) 839-8640
WWW.AUTHORHOUSE.COM

First published by AuthorHouse 02/01/05

ISBN: 1-4208-1262-9 (sc)

Printed in the United States of America
Bloomington, Indiana

This book is printed on acid-free paper.

FORWARD

My deepest desire is to be able to reach even one person with the strength and knowledge that the Lord gives us in time of need. To know from the innermost part of your being that He watches over us at all times. Not to push us thru life and lifes choices, but rather, to guide, protect, and give us wisdom in all decisions and trials that we might face. My strength comes from knowing that we shall all be home soon.

To my husband and my gift from God,

Brian for all your support. To my children John, Kelly, Andy and all my grandchildren, may the love, peace, and joy from the Lord fill your lives to overflowing.

In Jesus Name,
GranmaB

WHAT

DO YOU

NEED TO

KNOW ABOUT

TERRORISM

Grandma says,

The only thing you

R E A L L Y

need to know about

T E R R O R I S M

is

I will say of the Lord,

He is my refuge and my fortress:

MY GOD;

in him will I trust.

Psalm91

THOU SHALT NOT BE AFRAID

FOR THE TERROR BY NIGHT;

NOR FOR THE ARROW

THAT FLIETH BY DAY;

NOR FOR THE PESTILENCE

THAT WALKETH IN DARKNESS

NOR FOR THE DESTRUCTION

THAT WASTETH AT

NOONDAY.

PSALM 91:5,6

About the Author

Grandma B. (Becky Kunz) was born in Ohio. She moved to Nebraska as a young girl. There she grew up on a Midwest cattle farm. Later after graduating from High School she moved to Alaska, then on to Washington State where she now resides.

Being now a Grandmother of Eight, the questions asked of her by them concerning the issues that are facing our Nation and this world today, have inspires the answer in this book.

Her love for the Lord, and of life, Her Grandchildren, family and friends have all been supportive in writing of this book.

www.ingramcontent.com/pod-product-compliance
Lightning Source LLC
Chambersburg PA
CBHW050349290526
45785CB00006B/2693